COPING

GENDER DYSPHORIA

ROSE MCCARTHY

ROSEN PUBLISHING

Published in 2024 by The Rosen Publishing Group, Inc.
2544 Clinton Street, Buffalo, NY 14224

Portions of this work were originally authored by Ellen McGrody and published as *Coping with Gender Dysphoria*. All new material in this edition was authored by Rose McCarthy.

Designer: Rachel Rising
Editor: Corona Brezina

Library of Congress Cataloging-in-Publication Data

Names: McCarthy, Rose, author.
Title: Gender dysphoria / Rose McCarthy.
Description: Buffalo, NY : Rosen Publishing, [2023] | Series: Coping | Includes index.
Identifiers: LCCN 2023009753 (print) | LCCN 2023009754 (ebook) | ISBN 9781499474220 (library binding) | ISBN 9781499474213 (paperback) | ISBN 9781499474237 (ebook)
Subjects: LCSH: Gender identity--Juvenile literature. | Gender expression--Juvenile literature. | Gender identity disorders--Juvenile literature.
Classification: LCC HQ18.552 .M34 2023 (print) | LCC HQ18.552 (ebook) | DDC 305.3--dc23/eng/20230317
LC record available at https://lccn.loc.gov/2023009753
LC ebook record available at https://lccn.loc.gov/2023009754

Some of the images in this book illustrate individuals who are models. The depictions do not imply actual situations or events.

Manufactured in the United States of America

CPSIA Compliance Information: Batch #CSRYA24. For further information, contact Rosen Publishing at 1-800-237-9932.

CONTENTS

CHAPTER 1

WHAT IS GENDER DYSPHORIA?

Adolescence is a time of transformation and completion of rites of passage toward adulthood. For some young people, this stage of self-discovery includes coming to terms with gender identity. A person's gender identity is their internal sense of their own gender. They may express their gender identity outwardly through clothing choices, hair, makeup, mannerisms, and voice.

Gender doesn't always correspond with sex, which is determined by physical characteristics. Gender is a social construct. Some people are transgender, meaning that their gender identity does not match the sex they were assigned at birth. They may experience a condition called gender dysphoria, which is an incongruence between one's experienced gender and assigned sex, resulting in a strong desire and conviction to be another gender. Not everyone who is transgender experiences gender dysphoria, however, and not everyone who experiences gender dysphoria is transgender. Anyone, regardless of age, can experience gender dysphoria or identify as transgender. Gender dysphoria is very personal and can be intensified by different life circumstances.

To someone experiencing gender dysphoria, it feels like society is imposing a classification that doesn't match their innate sense of who they are.

For some people, solving gender dysphoria involves medical options. For others, merely adopting a new gender presentation can help, while some rely on therapy to help them feel more comfortable in their assigned gender. There is no single path to solving gender dysphoria that works for everyone, though there are strategies available for anyone to use.

Acceptance and support from family, friends, and peers can give trans people confidence as they explore their gender identity and gender expression.

GENDER IDENTITIES

The idea that all people can be labeled based on their physical traits at birth can create a lot of conflict. Those whose gender identity and expression align with the sex they were assigned at birth are considered cisgender. Those whose identity blurs the lines and rubs against the idea of a binary model are often considered transgender. The prefixes of these words—"trans" and "cis"—mean "opposite" and "on this side of" respectively.

People who were assigned male or female at birth but don't identify that way have many ways to express themselves as something other than a boy or a girl.

With this understanding, it's important to note that being transgender can mean a lot of different things. Imagine a color wheel. If what society typically defines as boys and girls are somewhere on that color wheel, there are other genders on the same wheel. Not everyone fits into this model, but it can be a helpful guide to understanding what gender can look like.

This idea is sometimes referred to as a gender spectrum, much like the color spectrum that makes up visible light. Similarly, someone can be a mix of different genders or identify as not having gender whatsoever. Therefore, being transgender can include people who are transitioning from one gender to another, people who express themselves as a certain gender some of the time, people who don't have a gender at all, and just about everyone else who does not fit easily into the binary model of gender. Some people who reject defining themselves as a specific gender may describe themselves with terms such as gender-fluid or nonbinary.

Gender means something to everyone. Even those who identify as cisgender have a gender identity, or an internal sense of gender. People express their gender identity through their behavior, clothing, hairstyle, voice, and body characteristics, all of which can be considered part of their gender expression. For example, if a person who was assigned male at birth grows up to express and identify as a boy, that means they are a cisgender boy. Understandings and expressions of gender can change over time, so there have been many ways to express gender throughout various cultures.

UNDERSTANDING GENDER DYSPHORIA

Gender can be fun to play with for some people while being challenging to navigate for others. Because gender is a form of self-expression, it can be exciting to express yourself in a way that's different from the norm. However, because gender is also associated with cultural expectations about people's bodies and their roles in society, someone's internal sense of who they are and how they express that to the world can be hard to safely explore. When someone feels confused or sad about the way gender is imposed on them, when they want very badly to be a different gender, or when they live in a culture that restricts certain kinds of gender expression, that can cause gender dysphoria. As of 2022, the American Psychiatric Association defines gender dysphoria as "psychological distress that results from an incongruence between one's sex assigned at birth and one's gender identity."

Many different elements can contribute to gender dysphoria. A person's upbringing, their nationality, their class, their race, their ability status, and other factors all play a role. Feminist theorist and legal scholar Kimberlé Crenshaw developed the theory of intersectionality to address the way someone's gender and race must be considered together to understand the oppressions they might face and the lives they might lead. Intersectionality is important to take into account when discussing gender dysphoria.

Not all transgender people experience gender dysphoria, but it's a common thread among many members of the trans community. Per a survey taken in 2022 by the Williams Institute at the

UCLA School of Law, there are estimated to be 1.6 million transgender people in the United States. Many transgender people are working to confront their own gender dysphoria and help others who experience it find strategies to overcome it. The primary struggle for transgender people throughout the world is how to express their real selves and be respected as such by society at large. This sort of self-expression is vital for transgender people to live full and healthy lives. For many, living that healthy life starts with addressing the symptoms of their gender dysphoria through the process of transition—referring to the physical, mental, and social act of expressing a gender identity that does not match the one assigned to them at birth.

People experience gender dysphoria differently depending on their particular culture's expectations of gender and the way they are treated by the people around them.

ADDRESSING GENDER DYSPHORIA

Gender dysphoria can cause significant damage to a person's well-being. It can lead to stress, cause rifts with a person's family and friends, and exacerbate existing mental and physical health issues. Finding strategies to manage gender dysphoria can help to ease symptoms like anxiety and depression. Many transgender people credit such strategies and the process of transition with helping them heal and find a new lease on life.

It's valuable to note that there is not one determined set of strategies that will work for all transgender people. Thanks to the lens of intersectionality, it's clear that the needs and backgrounds of transgender people throughout the world are different, and the strategies that work for one person's gender dysphoria will not necessarily work for everyone. Even steps as common as coming out as one's true gender and transitioning to that gender through medical and social means are not the ultimate path for everyone with gender dysphoria. Not everyone will feel good or safe in pursuing such a path.

Gender dysphoria can be frustrating and painful, but it's possible to come to terms with one's personal sense of gender. Each person's experience of gender dysphoria is unique, stemming from their own individuality as well as circumstances such as personal background and culture. Although there's no single path toward resolving the feeling of gender dysphoria, there are many strategies that people have used to address and overcome gender dysphoria.

Even if you don't believe that a certain approach will work for you, learning about other trans people's personal struggles and victories may help clarify your own thoughts and feelings. Plenty of people have succeeded in confronting gender dysphoria and achieving a sense of harmony between their identified gender, body, and self-expression. It might not be easy, but you can make the journey toward overcoming gender dysphoria as well.

It's vital to include and consider the needs of each individual when exploring how to treat and confront gender dysphoria symptoms.

MYTHS & FACTS

MYTH: Gender dysphoria is a mental illness.

FACT: In the past, the Diagnostic and Statistical Manual of Mental Disorders (DSM) listed "gender identity disorder" as a mental disorder. In 2013, the reference was updated and the diagnosis changed to "gender dysphoria," which focuses on the sense of distress caused by the condition. The change made it clear that gender dysphoria is not a psychological illness that can be "treated" by trying to force people with the diagnosis to become cisgender.

MYTH: All transgender people are gay.

FACT: Even though transgender people are included in the LGBTQ+ umbrella, gender identity and sexual orientation are different. Like cisgender people, transgender people can identify as a variety of different sexual orientations. They can be gay, straight, bisexual, or some other category.

MYTH: Some inclusive educational initiatives "groom" children to become gay or transgender.

FACT: Exposing young people to information about LGBTQ+ topics does not affect their sexual orientation or gender identity. Gender identity and sexual orientation are not easily changed. Educational materials on LGBTQ+ issues won't cause kids to become gay or transgender, and so-called conversion therapy intended to change sexual orientation or gender identity is ineffective and harmful.

Cisgender people can become allies by learning about how to support transgender and nonbinary people and treat them with respect.

CHAPTER 2

EXPRESSING GENDER

Cultural expectations regarding gender are deeply ingrained. Regardless of how open-minded they are, people generally expect that a baby will either be a boy or a girl. In school, work, social, and home settings, it's usually assumed that peers, coworkers, friends, and relatives present themselves either as masculine or feminine. Any other option is regarded as the exception. For some gender nonconforming people, standing out as different from everyone else in the crowd can be difficult. Others relish confounding societal expectations in asserting their gender identity. People managing gender dysphoria must navigate what forms of gender presentation they find the most authentic, appropriate, and comfortable.

GENDER PERCEPTION AND PRESENTATION

If someone feels pressured by societal expectations and relationships with people around them to act or look a certain way according to their assigned gender, that can cause dysphoria even if the person doesn't fully recognize it. Dysphoria is rarely explicit; it's uncommon for someone to recognize at first that the distress they're experiencing is related to the way they present themselves and are perceived. Often, dysphoria can come in the form of wanting to express oneself in a particular way without necessarily knowing why, or being jealous that other people are free to express themselves in a way that one feels restricted from.

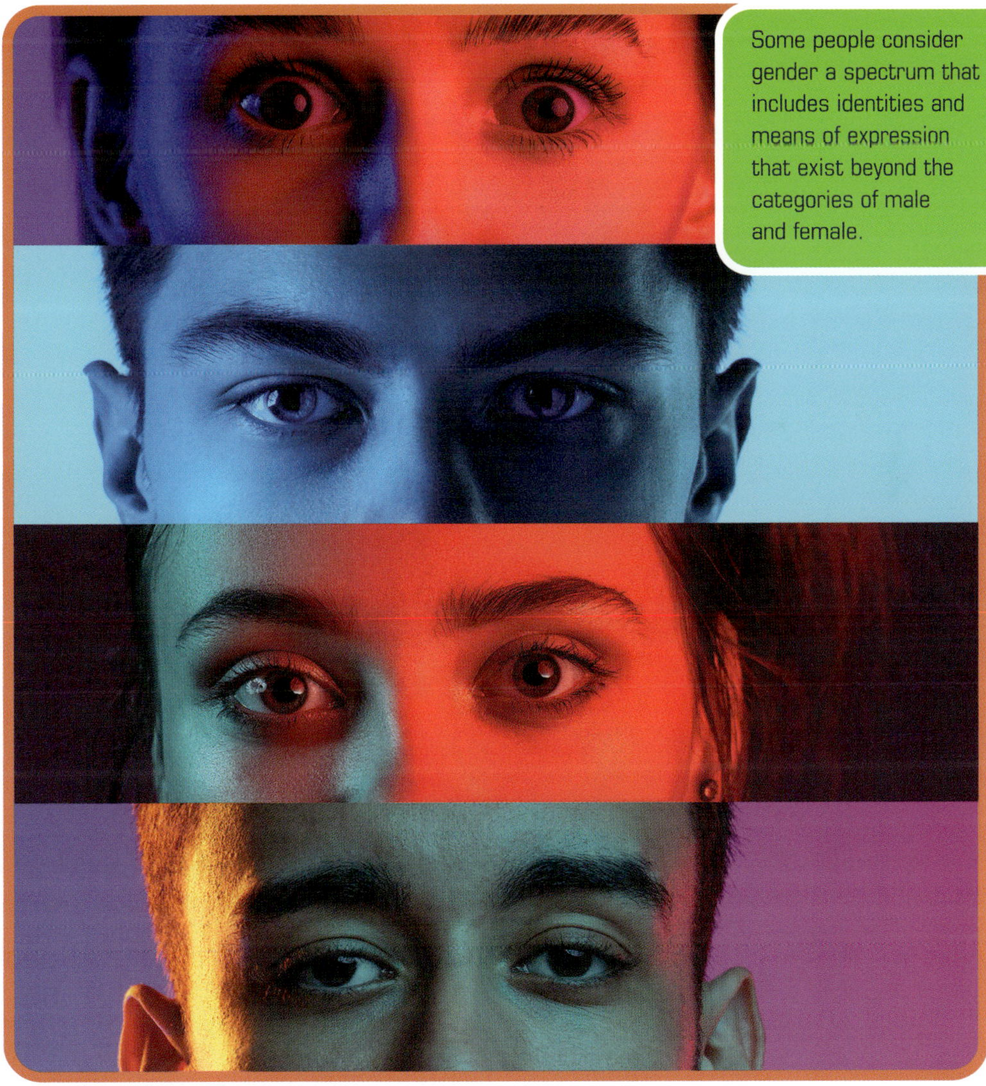

Some people consider gender a spectrum that includes identities and means of expression that exist beyond the categories of male and female.

For some, matching gendered perceptions can be incredibly validating. It can be great for some women, for example, to have the person in the mirror reflect what society believes a woman should look like. But perceptions aren't the entirety of what gender is. Someone can be a woman who loves watching sports and action movies and hates wearing makeup and still be a woman, if that's who they feel they are. Expressing identity is about expressing oneself authentically, without compromise.

It can be scary and overwhelming for a person to change the way they present themselves, and that sort of change can impact their relationships with others.

Consider a hypothetical person. They experience dysphoria because of the gender and sex that were assigned to them at birth. They don't like having to move about the world in a way that reflects the societal expectations attached to that gender. Resolving that conflict comes in several parts. For starters, they'll want to begin expressing themselves in a way that reflects who they want to be, rather than in a way that reflects who society believes they should be. They'll need to find strategies that make that kind of expression easy, safe, and manageable in a world that might not welcome subversion of gendered norms. Whether this means a transgender person who wants to present as a gender opposing the one they were assigned or a cisgender person looking to escape rigid social expectations, gender presentation can help someone find a way to show the world who they are.

ELEMENTS OF GENDER PRESENTATION

Changing one's gender presentation can take many forms. For some, it means changing the way they look, from clothing to hair and more. For others, it means changing the pronouns they use to refer to themselves and asking others to do the same. It can mean that someone chooses to go by a new name. Gender presentation can be a scary and daunting thing to change. It requires a lot of courage, a little creativity, and a supportive group of friends or family.

It's vital to remember that while many people with gender dysphoria choose to incorporate changing their gender presentation into their transition, this isn't going to be the preferred path for everyone, nor is it the only way to manage gender dysphoria. For many, presenting as a gender that wasn't assigned to them at birth isn't feasible or safe. Cost, legal restrictions, familial situations, abusive relationships, cultural expectations, and many other factors can impede someone from presenting their gender the way that they want. Finding strategies to confront such obstacles and supporting people who do so is hugely important.

PICKING PRONOUNS

For many transgender people, choosing new pronoun combinations is a milestone in their journey toward resolving gender dysphoria. Some transgender people may decide to switch from using "she/her" to "he/him," for example. Many nonbinary people opt for gender-neutral pronouns such as "they/them." The Human Rights Campaign provides an explanation of newer, less common pronouns: www.hrc.org/resources/understanding-neopronouns.

For many transgender people, their choice of pronouns represents an important element in their gender identity. When family and friends use their chosen pronouns naturally, it signals acceptance of a transgender person's gender identity. Failure to use accurate pronouns can be either an honest mistake or a sign of hostility. If someone uses the wrong pronoun, correct them and explain that it's hurtful to be misgendered. Show respect to the people around you by asking about their personal pronouns and sharing your own pronouns when you're introduced.

Gender presentation can take someone from wishing they looked a certain way to actually appearing that way. For some, this can include binding (the act of using restrictive clothing to bind one's breasts and create a flat appearance) or tucking (which refers to hiding traditionally male-assigned genitalia using special undergarments and other tools). For others, this means learning how to use or abandoning the use of makeup, cutting or growing their hair, training their voice to be higher or lower, or collecting a new wardrobe. Some people choose to use medical interventions to make these acts of gender presentation easier.

Supporting the gender that someone identifies as is vital. That includes honoring their choices and respecting their pronouns.

OBSTACLES TO CHANGE

An important part of expressing one's identity fully is finding a name that feels good. Deciding on a name that feels right is a powerful tool in affirming one's identity. Names and pronouns can change over time, but they should always be respected by others. Many transgender people refer to the names given to them by their parents as their "deadnames." For those people, hearing their deadname can cause significant dysphoria and a lot of psychological pain. Thus, many choose not to share or ask about details of a person's assigned identity, no matter the context.

A lot of transgender people go to great lengths to ensure their gender identity and expression are acknowledged throughout their lives. They communicate their need for respect to others through actions like changing their name legally and working to have their name and gender recognized by family, friends, classmates, and colleagues. For some, this also means working with their schools or workplaces to use the correct restroom facility safely or wear a uniform more befitting their gender identity.

People who attempt to change their name and gender can face opposition from peers, governments, and employers. There has been progress for some. For example, in December 2016, New York issued its first intersex birth certificate to Sara Kelly Keenan, acknowledging Sara's identity and status as neither male nor female. In 2018, California became the first state to issue nonbinary birth certificates, and over a dozen states have adopted the policy. More than 20 states allow people to choose an "x" rather than a specific gender on their driver's license as well. However, in 2022, Oklahoma became the first state to explicitly ban nonbinary gender markers on birth certificates. Despite progress, transgender people continue to face obstacles and opposition in having their identities acknowledged.

For transgender teens, the support of family and friends can be critical when they're struggling with gender dysphoria and establishing their gender identity.

Policies and politics may get in the way of a person's goals, but supportive communities and alternative means of gender presentation can help someone subvert such challenges. Some transgender people only present their identities in safe spaces, such as online communities or support groups. Some choose to live a stressful "double life," adopting their true identities where it's safe and wearing their assigned identities like a mask where it's not. Many transgender people are forced to deadname and misgender themselves in procedural settings just to get by.

This can mean applying for jobs under a long-incorrect name or presenting themselves differently in government buildings. Finding ways to balance someone's actual identity and the unfortunate necessity of maintaining their previous self is crucial to ultimately achieving gender harmony.

Those who don't face as many risks and barriers will often choose to "come out," asserting their gender identity throughout all aspects of life. Many of these people aim to completely blend in as the gender they are presenting, without the risk of anyone seeing them as their assigned gender. In the transgender community, this is commonly called passing. Passing can be important because it mitigates various risks that come with presenting as a gender that doesn't match the sex a person was assigned. Those risks include psychological damage, physical harm, and legal implications, all considered forms of transphobia.

While someone's gender doesn't hinge upon the opinions of other people, passing can feel extremely validating for transgender people and others with gender dysphoria.

Making decisions regarding gender presentation is a key factor in resolving gender dysphoria. You'll feel more confident if your physical appearance and sense of style correspond with your gender identity. Expressing your gender identity can improve your mental health and sense of self-worth. And there's no right or wrong way to assert your gender presentation. Many people prefer to pass as the gender they're presenting, but others, such as nonbinary and gender-fluid people, consider it less important. Deciding how to communicate your gender identity to others can be an ongoing process, and some aspects, such as changing your name, can be challenging. In the end, though, most transgender people consider overcoming such obstacles to be worth the hassle.

CHAPTER 3

MEDICAL OPTIONS

For some people experiencing gender dysphoria, medical treatment is necessary in order for them to accept their physical appearance. They may seek hormone treatment and gender affirmation surgeries that will masculinize or feminize their bodies. People can experience considerable stress due to gender dysphoria that affects their mental health and quality of life. Medical treatment that affirms their gender identity can make them more confident in their gender expression. Many people experiencing gender dysphoria feel more comfortable in their own bodies when their physical traits match the cultural perceptions of their gender identity. Medical therapies can help them achieve this outcome.

AFFIRMING GENDER

The medical treatments employed to help confront dysphoria and allow people to have bodies that more accurately reflect social expectations of their gender identity have been standardized over time. The 2015 U.S. Transgender Survey found that a clear majority of transgender respondents sought medical care as part of their transition, with 78 percent of respondents wanting to incorporate hormone therapy, 77 percent wanting mental health care, and 25 percent having undergone some form of transition-related surgery.

Doctors throughout the world have been employing strategies like these to help transgender people since the early 1900s. The World Professional Association for Transgender Health (WPATH) maintains that gender-affirming treatments "play an undisputed role in contributing toward favorable outcomes" and are proven to improve the lives of those with gender dysphoria.

Medical options can be an important means of helping someone tackle gender dysphoria and be more comfortable in their own skin.

It has been said in the past that transgender people are "born in the wrong body." While this is generally considered inappropriate and doesn't reflect the experiences of everyone, it can be an accurate way for some people to articulate their experiences and their feelings. Many would prefer to have been born with different physical traits, some of which can be induced by rewiring the body to produce a kind of hormone that aligns with their gender identity. Others can be introduced by means of various surgeries.

IDENTITY DOCUMENTS

Obtaining a driver's license with your correct gender can be as easy as filling out a simple form that requires marking M, F, or X. Or it can be a difficult process that requires proof of surgery, a court order, or an amended birth certificate. It depends on which state you live in. In over 20 states, changing your legal gender on identity documents is a straightforward process. In the others, it can be either slightly more complicated or nearly impossible. Some states require documents such as proof of surgery, for example, even though not all transgender people choose gender-affirming surgery. Obtaining an amended birth certificate can be even more difficult in some states, and a few have no provision for amending gender. In addition, the fees can be a barrier to obtaining accurate identity documents. Resources such as the Transgender Law Center provide information and resources on legally changing name and gender.

HORMONE THERAPY

Hormone therapy is a common means of addressing dysphoria about the body. It's the way that many begin the process of transitioning. When employed alongside strategies like changing gender presentation, it can help make the social and legal parts of transition easier. This sort of medical transition can be started at any stage in life. Its effects and the medications used will vary from person to person. Often, the kind of treatment that works for someone is dependent on their age and assigned sex.

There are several ways to administer hormones as part of a transition. Generally, the treatment pursued hinges on a person's assigned sex and physical makeup. Bodies that are assigned female at birth typically produce estrogenic hormones in the estrone family of steroids, like estrogen, while bodies that are assigned male typically produce androgenic hormones and steroids, including testosterone.

For example, if someone assigned male at birth identifies as a girl, they may want to pursue treatment that makes their body more in line with the body of someone who would be assigned female at birth. In that case, treatment would involve medications (known as antiandrogens) that block the production of anabolic steroids, such as testosterone. Estrogenic hormones, like estradiol and progesterone, would also be added. These medications can be taken through external patches, gels, pills, and injections. Sometimes the way hormones are ingested and the amount given changes based on the trajectory of a person's transition.

Consider someone who was assigned female at birth, identifies as nonbinary, and wants the world at large to perceive them as typically masculine. Hormone therapy can help because, for that person, the application of testosterone can help end monthly periods, reduce the prominence of their breasts, and encourage facial and body hair growth, in addition to naturally lowering the pitch of their voice. All of this can help the person move about the world in a way that's more reflective of their identity while making them more comfortable in their own skin.

Studies have shown that most young people who suppress puberty choose to continue gender-affirming treatments.

Those beginning hormone therapy at a younger age may require a different set of therapies than others. The body doesn't start producing sex hormones until puberty, which begins around age 10 for those assigned female at birth and around age 11 for those assigned male. Medications called puberty blockers can prevent and delay puberty. This gives young people time to make decisions about gender identity without having to worry about the hormones produced during puberty permanently transforming their bodies.

GENDER AFFIRMATION SURGERIES

Hormone therapies can only do so much. While they can influence the development of breasts or body hair and impact mood and emotions, they often don't cause all of the changes a transgender person may desire. The gaps left by hormone therapy don't bother everyone, but for those who are looking for more, there are many surgical options available to continue the transition process. Unlike hormone therapy, access to these surgeries can be limited by access to regional care and the occasional necessity of letters of support from other health care providers. In some places, such surgeries can be necessary for changing legal documentation as well.

Gender affirmation surgery can be very fulfilling for many and necessary for obtaining legal identity documents for some.

As with hormone therapy, the surgeries someone chooses to undergo are usually determined by their assigned sex. For those who were assigned male at birth, the surgeries typically used include vaginoplasty, in which a doctor reshapes traditionally male genitalia like the penis and testicles into a vagina; orchiectomy, a surgery which removes a person's testicles; breast enhancement, which usually acts in addition to breast growth promoted by hormone therapy; facial feminization surgery, in which the face is augmented to have a more traditionally feminine appearance; and trachea shaving, which reduces the appearance of the Adam's apple on the neck and can heighten the pitch of one's voice. Those surgeries are usually accompanied by hair removal techniques such as laser or electrolysis, as hormones alone can't completely cease the growth of facial and body hair in most people.

For those assigned female at birth, available surgeries include mastectomy—the removal of breasts in order to give the chest a flat appearance—and phalloplasty, which describes the construction of a penis in place of traditionally female genitalia. Testosterone is far more aggressive than estrogen, so trans masculine individuals and transgender men usually will not require surgeries focused on modifying their faces or their voices.

OBSTACLES TO CARE

While most medical organizations endorse guidelines for transgender health care and doctors generally adhere to and support people based on those guidelines, many trans people do not get the medical care they need and deserve. The 2015 U.S. Transgender Survey reported that 55 percent of those who sought coverage for transition-related surgeries were denied, and 25 percent of those who sought hormone coverage were denied. The survey also shows that 33 percent of those who saw a doctor in the previous year had negative experiences related to their gender identity, 23 percent of respondents had difficulty seeing a doctor at all due to fear of mistreatment, and 33 percent did not visit a doctor because of barriers regarding cost.

Some doctors will go as far as obstructing care. Their negative attitudes toward transgender people and their belief that cisgender identities are more valid informs their perspective and drives them to block transgender individuals from treatment. Doctors may also perform conversion therapies that seek to "cure" them into being cisgender. Those with gender dysphoria should never have to educate their doctors, though the unfortunate truth is that not all people are going to have access to compassionate coverage, and they must rely on the help of their communities to get the health care and therapy they need.

Organizations such as WPATH and University of California San Francisco's Center of Excellence for Transgender Health maintain guidelines for treatment. WPATH's highly regarded Standards of Care provides direction for health care professionals and informs several insurance companies in the United States.

Support groups and online communities, such as MyTransHealth, dedicate themselves to helping transgender people find resources, and

Finding transgender communities on social networks can provide a sense of reassurance to someone who doesn't have access to a supportive health care provider.

many transgender people report having heard about treatment options by word of mouth. LGBTQ+ law organizations like Lambda Legal sometimes maintain resources concerning equal access to health care. In addition, many cities and schools run LGBTQ+ and gay/straight alliance organizations that can help people find resources.

Legal barriers to care can include state health care policies and age requirements for treatment. Most state Medicaid programs, for example, do not cover transition-related health care, though patients in a few states have found success in getting this coverage. The legal age of consent for any kind of medical care, including transition-related care, can vary from place to place, and minors often require parental or guardian consent unless they are emancipated from their parents or such care is ordered by a court. The same resources that provide health care advice will often have advice regarding legal barriers too.

People's gender identities are about more than body parts, and medical therapies won't necessarily resolve all symptoms of gender dysphoria. Counseling can help people work on self-acceptance and address their gender identity concerns. Having a support system of family and friends can be invaluable for someone sorting out gender dysphoria. But some people feel the greatest relief through medical treatment of certain physical traits. In these cases, having access to care can be transformative. When there are barriers to obtaining care, being able to find support and resources related to health care needs can be critical to managing gender dysphoria.

CHAPTER 4

OVERCOMING PREJUDICE

Gender dysphoria is a difficult personal issue to manage, and the experience can be made even worse by societal pressures such as discrimination, prejudice, and misconceptions about trans people. For example, a friend might make a careless, hurtful remark that demonstrates harmful stereotypes about trans people. Some employers promote LGBTQ+ friendly policies, but others disregard when transgender people encounter hostility or harassment at workplaces. Likewise, many transgender students do not feel safe in their schools. The fight for transgender equality in public life is ongoing, as many states introduce laws and policies that restrict opportunities and basic rights for transgender people.

TRANSPHOBIA AND CISSEXISM

Transphobia refers to language and behavior that seeks to belittle, diminish, erase, or harm transgender people. This can include everything from laws that block transgender people from using public facilities to violence enacted against transgender people throughout the world. Cissexism is the primary driver of transphobia. It's the idea that cisgender people—their identities, their bodies, their experiences—are somehow more valid, valuable, or important than transgender people.

What does cissexism look like? How does transphobia harm transgender people? Cissexism is at play when a politician writes a bill proposing that bathrooms be assigned by "chromosomes at birth," or the "sex assigned on a person's birth certificate." It happens when an airport security checkpoint features a body scanner with two buttons, a pink button and a blue button, subjecting anyone whose bodies don't align with these vague categories to invasive pat downs and body searches.

Cissexism promotes a rigid system in which gender and sex are intrinsically linked and can never be questioned or modified.

Risks are introduced when a transgender person is perceived as visibly trans, or clocked; when they're referred to by their assigned sex and the wrong pronoun, or misgendered; and when they're called by the name they were given at birth, or deadnamed. These all fall under the umbrella of microaggressions, a term used to describe dismissive insults directed at a member of a minority group.

Unlike more blatant forms of transphobia, microaggressions can be subtle and even unintentional. Nevertheless, microaggressions betray an ingrained cissexism that the person committing them might not even be aware of. Telling someone that they are "pretty for a trans woman," asking personal questions about a person's medical, romantic, or sexual history, or offering unsolicited advice about how to look more "like a man" are all examples of transphobic microaggressions.

In addition to amplifying dysphoria, transphobia can expose gender-variant individuals to further hardships. The 2015 U.S. Transgender Survey reported high rates of harassment, economic hardship, employment instability, and homelessness in the trans population, all stemming from transphobia. Nearly half of respondents, for example, reported having been verbally harassed in the past year. Transphobia has also led to transgender people being denied access to public restroom facilities and prohibited from playing sports on teams aligned to their gender identities. Legislation has barred discussion of some LGBTQ+ topics in schools. Access to health care coverage for transgender people, particularly gender-affirming care for children, has been restricted. About one in ten respondents to the 2015 U.S. Transgender Survey reported having been denied access to a restroom in the prior year, with many more reporting having to avoid using a public restroom.

Everyone's individual story with transphobia is different. According to the 2015 U.S. Transgender Survey, transgender people rely on a variety of sources of support. Of those who reported their experiences with coming out, 60 percent found support from their families, 68 percent found support from their coworkers, and 56 percent found support from their classmates. This kind of support is hugely beneficial, with family support playing a key role in maintaining economic stability, ensuring access to health care, avoiding homelessness, and staving off psychological distress, including thoughts of suicide.

The path to acceptance isn't always easy, particularly for young people, but the support of family and friends provides invaluable reassurance and stability.

FAMILY HOSTILITY

It's not uncommon for families to be hostile or abusive to transgender family members or to refuse or be resistant to recognizing their gender, pronouns, or name. An upsetting 10 percent of respondents to the U.S. Transgender Survey reported a family member being violent toward them, and 8 percent reported being kicked out of their homes and pushed into homelessness. Some families will even push young people into harmful conversion therapies and force them to hide their identities even after coming out.

This kind of abuse can occur in romantic relationships as well. Nobody has to stay in an abusive relationship, for any reason. Many people, particularly those made more vulnerable by intersectional oppression, feel pressured to do so for several reasons, which include avoiding homelessness and attaining financial security. Know that there are organizations that can help vulnerable lesbian, gay, bisexual, transgender, and other queer people escape abusive situations. The National Domestic Violence Hotline acts as an always-available resource for those looking for help in abusive family, roommate, or romantic situations, and it maintains a list of resources specifically catering to LGBTQ+ people.

DISCRIMINATION AT WORK AND SCHOOL

Outside of the home, transgender people can face difficulty in school and at work. Many transgender students and workers face transphobia and cissexism from their classmates, coworkers, teachers, managers, and school leadership. In school, cissexism maintains rigid binary dress codes, and gendered bathrooms, locker rooms, and sports teams, while supporting a curriculum that ignores the existence of transgender people. Transphobia can leave transgender students struggling to have their identities recognized by school administration and fighting for recognition on their own.

Some people are hesitant to live openly as transgender at their workplace, where they can be subjected to discrimination and harassment.

Finding support from individual classmates, teachers, counselors, and administrators can be a big step forward for many. Organizations like the Transgender Law Center and Lambda Legal have published guides that help transgender students and their allied educators advocate for change. Classmates have come together to support their peers, through protest and using organizations like Gay, Lesbian and Straight Education Network (GLSEN) and Genders & Sexualities Alliance (GSA) Network to collect resources for themselves and educators alike. While it can be a struggle, it's more than possible to foster positivity, celebrate queer history, and found campus organizations dedicated to educating and protecting lesbian, gay, bisexual, transgender, and other queer students.

At work, transgender people of all ages face similar issues. Many face harassment from managers, coworkers, customers, and clients. According to the National Center for Transgender Equality, more than one in four transgender people have lost their jobs

Young people can demonstrate support for transgender rights by learning about issues transgender people face and treating their transgender peers with respect.

ANTI-TRANSGENDER VIOLENCE

The threat of violence against transgender people is very real. In 2021, the Human Rights Campaign reported that at least 50 transgender people were the victims of fatal violence in the United States. The actual number may be higher because victims are sometimes misgendered or not reported as transgender in official reports. A 2021 study by the Williams Institute at UCLA School of Law found that transgender people are more than four times likelier than cisgender people to experience violent victimization.

Anti-transgender bias was a factor in some of these cases. The Human Rights Campaign points out that for transgender people overall, "anti-transgender stigma, denial of opportunity and increased risk factors compound to create a culture of violence." Because of discrimination and lack of opportunities, transgender people are more likely to be forced into situations where they're at a greater risk of violence, such as homelessness, poverty, and unemployment. Transgender people also report experiencing discrimination from services such as homeless shelters or law enforcement when they try to ask for help.

because of transphobia, while more than 75 percent have experienced other discrimination in the workplace. At work, trans people may contend with bathroom use issues, gendered uniforms, potential violence, and exclusive insurance policies. They can end up fighting even to get hired, risking potential privacy violations, and confronting laws that don't protect them from employment discrimination.

STAYING SAFE

Many transgender and gender nonconforming people experience harassment—and sometimes even violence—just walking down the street. Changing legal documentation can be time-consuming and expensive. But without documentation, trans people are often exposed to a lack of legal protections and discrimination at the hands of police. Transgender immigrants are also impacted by oppression and discrimination from Border Patrol agents and misplaced in gendered detention centers, where they can be mistreated and denied care.

For transgender people, the mere act of staying safe can be stressful and exhausting. The threats can be institutional, political, and personal. When they face discrimination and harassment at work or school, transgender people advocate for LGBTQ+ friendly policies. When they're threatened by legislation proposing to take away rights such as accessing health care and obtaining accurate IDs, they lobby for increased protections. When they're rejected by family and friends, they turn to communities of like-minded people. When trans people become victims of violence, they're forced to consider measures such as carrying rape alarms, taking self-defense classes, or traveling in groups for safety. Anybody struggling with gender dysphoria should be clear-eyed about the difficulties of living openly as transgender. But there's also a strong, caring community ready to offer support.

Workplaces can become more welcoming to transgender employees by instituting formal LGBTQ+ inclusion policies and providing equality and diversity training.

CHAPTER 5

MENTAL HEALTH ISSUES

Although gender dysphoria is related to one's physical body, the anguish it causes is psychological. Gender dysphoria can contribute to other mental health issues, such as anxiety and depression, as well. Experiences such as transphobia and lack of support in one's personal life can further contribute to psychological distress. Transgender people in general are at a higher risk of anxiety, depression, and other mental health conditions. Practicing good self-care can help manage stress and anxiety. There are also mental health providers who specialize in gender identity who have the experience and expertise to treat gender dysphoria and related issues.

WHEN DYSPHORIA BECOMES OVERWHELMING

Note that this section will discuss suicide and self-harm.

It's hard to overstate the importance of mental health care when talking about gender dysphoria. When the news and various studies talk about transgender people, discussion of suicide risk and depression is quickly attached. It's important to make one thing clear: There are people within the transgender community who are scared, vulnerable, and think about and sometimes do things that can put their lives in danger. It can be a hard thing to talk about, but being open and honest about negative feelings and thoughts is an incredibly important first step toward getting the help needed to cope with these challenges and begin the healing process.

Confronting gender dysphoria head-on and taking steps to transition can help strengthen self-acceptance in order to pull away from darkness.

Ensuring transgender people are truly healthy starts by building a bridge from fear to openness when it comes to mental health issues. The 2015 U.S. Transgender Survey says 40 percent of transgender people have attempted suicide in their lifetimes, nearly nine times the attempted suicide rate in the general U.S. population. But even one person considering, attempting, or dying by suicide is too many and should be enough to make this issue important and worth discussing. Outside of suicide, some transgender people will self-harm through drug and alcohol abuse or through self-mutilation. Remember that people affected by thoughts of suicide or engaging in self-harm behavior need patience, understanding, and care.

Transgender people experience mental health stress from outside factors such as discrimination, as well as inner sources, such as gender dysphoria.

Many transgender people experience feelings of loneliness, especially if they feel they can't share their gender identity with family or friends for fear of rejection.

Many transgender people, their friends, their colleagues, and their families can tell stories of people they've lost and relay experiences concerning self-harm. Transgender people often fight from the margins to get help managing their gender dysphoria, and sometimes, the fight becomes overwhelming. The first step is knowing how to get help. The second is taking that knowledge and using it to help someone else. Trans people and their allies fight hard to get better, every single day, at talking to each other about depression and the risk of suicide and how to help connect those who are struggling with the resources they need.

IN TIMES OF CRISIS

If you're experiencing a crisis, there are resources that can offer immediate support. These can help you if you're considering self-harm, having mental health issues, or feeling threatened.

- **Trevor Lifeline**
  1-866-488-7386 I *www.thetrevorproject.org/get-help/#tt* A hotline to a crisis counselor for LGBTQ+ people ages 13 to 24 who are thinking about self-harm.

- **Trans Lifeline**
  1-877-565-8860 I *translifeline.org/hotline/*
  A hotline staffed by transgender people for transgender people in crisis or in need of support.

- **LGBT National Help Center**
  www.lgbthotline.org Offers several hotlines and chat resources providing support on issues related to sexual orientation and gender identity.

- **National Sexual Assault Hotline**
  1-800-656-HOPE (4673) I *www.rainn.org*
  A hotline offering confidential support and resources for people experiencing sexual assault or violence.

Don't hesitate to reach out to a friend or a hotline if you find yourself in crisis. You can get through the situation, and there are people out there who want to help you.

Talking about the risk of suicide is the hardest part of confronting gender dysphoria, but it's not the only mental health issue that dysphoria can cause. Being more aware of the mental health challenges that come with dysphoria can improve people's lives—and even save lives.

Reaching out for help can mean calling a friend for a chat or contacting a hotline serving people experiencing a crisis.

Even the most well-adjusted transgender person will struggle due to societal challenges, and preexisting mental health issues further complicate the situation.

DIVERSE TRANSGENDER PATHS

Dealing with dysphoria—and transphobia—can be incredibly hard and can affect every aspect of a person's life, including mental health. That means potentially causing and exacerbating various mental health conditions, including anxiety, depression, and post-traumatic stress disorder (PTSD). It also means that people who were born neurodivergent, like those with bipolar disorder and those on the autism spectrum, will have interactions with dysphoria and being transgender that look different from the experiences of neurotypical people.

Experiencing neurodivergence does not define a person, nor does it make them or their experiences any less valuable. In the trans community, people experiencing various degrees of mental health issues are common, with only 10 percent of respondents to the 2015 U.S. Transgender Survey reporting that psychological distress had not interfered with their life in any way in the past 30 days. That's why talking about mental health care and managing mental health issues are so important when addressing gender dysphoria. Transgender youth face unique challenges that can affect their mental health, and identifying sources of distress can help them advocate for their needs and build resilience.

Many transgender people attest that transitioning helps them confront these issues. A respondent to the 2015 U.S. Transgender Survey told this story well, saying, “I spent decades torturing myself into depression because I was certain that coming out would destroy my life. I did everything I could to get my transness to go away but it left me psychologically weak, and on the verge of suicide.” For people like this, embracing who they are is a crucial part of healing. The survey data shows that the rate of psychological distress experienced by transgender people falls tremendously as time passes from the beginning of their transition.

Transition alone won’t solve mental health issues for everyone. In the case of those born neurodivergent, supporting mental health is a pervasive theme throughout their lives. Transphobia, and the violence and instability that come with it, can exacerbate mental health issues no matter how long someone has been in transition.

The steps that a person takes to transition represent a highly personal decision and a journey that can improve their outlook on life.

MENTAL HEALTH AND SELF CARE

Pursuing regular mental health care is the way forward for many and can become a vital part of someone's transition. Self-care means seeking out techniques for healing and crisis management that can be done on the fly at home, at school, and everywhere else. Self-care can be vital for managing symptoms of stress and anxiety, such as panic attacks. Relaxation techniques such as deep breathing, meditation, and yoga can make a big difference. Community websites like the Trevor Project and Trans Lifeline provide ideas for self-care.

Self-care can be as broad as seeking out a mental health care professional and as small as taking a shower. Small, gratifying things, every single day, can make a huge difference. Listening to music, exercising, eating a healthy diet, sleeping, wearing favorite clothes, reading, playing games, hanging out with friends—in times of crisis, even small moments of positivity turn a lot of effort into emotional reward.

Therapists, psychologists, and psychiatrists can be helpful, though not all providers understand transgender experiences. Finding trans-affirming mental health care can be difficult and scary, but ultimately very rewarding. Sites like MyTransHealth help people throughout the United States find all kinds of trans-affirming medical care, including mental health care. Many schools have on-campus mental health professionals who may be able to provide access to queer-friendly care.

Check out resources offered by local support groups. Some queer centers provide services such as counseling, workshops, community events, and training programs.

It's important that transgender people take their mental health concerns seriously. If you're a transgender person experiencing gender dysphoria and other issues, remind yourself that good mental health is essential to your overall well-being. Even if you don't think you're in danger of spiraling into crisis, addressing mental health concerns can improve your confidence and quality of life. Accessing quality care may be a challenge, but it's worth the struggle. The path toward mental health wellness is different for everyone, and you can reach a place where your gender dysphoria and other issues are under control.

CHAPTER 6

BUILDING CONNECTIONS

Transgender people who feel a need for connection can reach out to find other people who understand their struggles and desires. The transgender community is inclusive, diverse, and welcoming. They are accepting of individuals of all creeds, colors, and backgrounds, from anywhere in the world. There are plenty of people who are willing to share their wisdom and personal experiences with newcomers. Transgender people have a long history of coming together to fight stigma and discrimination. If you're a transgender person feeling lost and hopeless, the transgender community can assure you that things will get better.

ACCEPTANCE AND RESILIENCE

The transgender community is one that fights for itself. Many of the groups and foundations that work to further the cause of transgender welfare were founded by people under the transgender umbrella. In addition, transgender people have long been at the forefront of the fight for rights not just for those who are trans, but also for all queer-aligned people.

One of the biggest misconceptions about transgender people is that being trans and experiencing gender dysphoria are modern phenomena. Cultural history shows that isn't true. While Western cultures have had a longstanding binary gender system, many other cultures allowed space for gender exploration before colonization and capitalism made that harder. In Native American traditions, for example, a Two-Spirit person is someone who embodies the spiritual presence of both men and women. In another example, fa'afafinc are a gender-variant group in the Samoan tradition who choose to embody masculine and feminine gender traits and perform traditionally feminine duties in the home.

Growing acceptance, visibility, and access to technology has made the struggle for trans rights easier and provided new access to resources all over the globe.

Learning about these histories can be challenging, as the forces of cissexism fight to delegitimize the identities of transgender people. Even though gender nonconforming people have existed for generations, institutional information about trans experience is limited. The information that does circulate does so thanks to intracommunity efforts. Transgender people and their allies rely on each other to spread knowledge and inspire change.

The transgender community is strong, welcoming, and diverse. Many transgender people are willing to connect with young adults reaching out for guidance.

For an individual experiencing gender dysphoria, it might seem that nobody else can understand their suffering, but it can help to reach out to others in the same situation.

BUILDING CONNECTIONS

The experience of gender dysphoria is deeply personal and can be very isolating, but no one is alone in their struggle. There are millions of transgender people throughout the world who have experienced the same feelings. Trans people can often feel isolated in their struggle, some in their desire to wake up in another body, others in their feeling of being lost in a maze of social expectations. Connecting with people who share the experience of being transgender or having dysphoria can be incredibly fulfilling. It can also help those looking to understand the condition of gender dysphoria find answers and allies in their journey of knowledge.

Transgender people and their allies have access to more communities than ever before. The LGBTQ+ movement has spurred the existence of queer community centers in schools and cities around the globe. National organizations, like the Human Rights Campaign and the National Center for Transgender Equality, dedicate themselves to providing resources and institutional advocacy for trans and queer people. Groups like the Transgender Law Center, Lambda Legal, and the American Civil Liberties Union work tirelessly to defend transgender people in court.

Outside of national organizations, transgender people are banding together in places around the United States and throughout the world. Many cities have trans lady picnics, trans support groups, and youth-specific groups. Organizations like PFLAG seek to rally and educate families of queer people together. There are hundreds of opportunities to find community. There are hackathons, such as Trans*H4CK; queer camps, such as the University of California's yearly T-Camp; magazines and periodicals, such as Duke University's *Transgender Studies Quarterly*; and game conventions, such as the Queerness and Games Conference and GaymerX, all dedicated to exposing trans exceptionalism and providing community and healing.

Some camps specifically support transgender youth. Activities may include traditional outdoor camp experiences along with programs exploring issues such as gender identity and building community.

Talking to community members in real life and seeking printed, published resources is a good way to find communities that are safe and trustworthy.

There are also many celebrations of trans identity, history, and resilience that happen worldwide every single year. Pride parades are the largest expression of this. Along with Pride, events like Transgender Awareness Month, which happens every November, seek to give transgender people and their allies a platform from which to talk about their needs. Transgender Day of Visibility, founded by activist Rachel Crandall-Crocker in 2009, occurs each year on March 31 to celebrate trans people and raise awareness. Transgender Day of Remembrance, on November 20, is an international day of action that has honored the lives of trans people lost to suicide and violence since 1999.

Social media can be an important tool for finding resources and friends for trans youth, especially those outside of urban areas. Trans communities on Reddit, Instagram, Twitter, and YouTube can be a safe way to make connections and seek information. Searching for tags concerning gender dysphoria and being transgender can be a great way to start. In exploring online resources, self-care is advised, as there can be harassment in online spaces and not everything read online should be trusted.

For many, finding a loving partner or partners and sharing closeness with someone is really important and very special. Transgender people, like their cisgender counterparts, can identify as many different sexual orientations. Transgender people can be gay, straight, bisexual, asexual, demisexual, demiromantic, and anything in between. They fall in love and are loved by other trans people and cis people alike.

Safe relationship practices are as important for transgender people as they are for anyone else, if not more so due to increased rates of relationship abuse, HIV, and other sexually transmitted diseases in the trans population. Remember that no one deserves to be in a harmful relationship and that there are resources like the National Domestic Abuse Hotline that can help. As for everyone, it's important to practice safe sex by using condoms and birth control to avoid the transmission of disease and avert unintended pregnancy. While hormones have an impact on the ability of some transgender people to procreate, it's still wise to practice safe sex always and regularly talk to a doctor about sexual activity and STD testing.

Gender dysphoria is distressing and even frightening for many young people. It can be disorienting, confusing, and hurtful to have society view and label you in a way that doesn't match your own sense of who you are. For many people, resolving gender dysphoria is a personal journey that is stressful and complicated. But there are resources available that provide support to transgender people as they overcome gender dysphoria and explore their gender identity.

It's vital to help trans people feel accepted, navigate the complexities of gender identity and gender expression, and find a way forward. Those who identify as transgender often needed an incredible amount of courage, strength, and support to express their identity to the world. They know who they are and deserve acceptance. It may not be easy to cope with the difficulties of gender dysphoria, but coming to terms with your gender identity and gender expression can ultimately be highly fulfilling.

For some transgender people, presenting a gender expression that reflects their gender identity is a significant milestone in their personal journey.

10 GREAT QUESTIONS TO ASK A SCHOOL ADMINISTRATOR

1. Does the school have equity and inclusion policies that address the needs of transgender students?

2. Does the school have an anti-bullying policy that specifies protections for LGBTQ+ students?

3. Would a transgender student at this school have access to restrooms, locker rooms, sports teams, activities, or uniforms that align with their gender identity and expression?

4. Have educators been trained in providing a safe environment for LGBTQ+ students?

5. Does the school have any LGBTQ+ organizations, such as a gay/straight alliance?

6. Who is the school's Title IX coordinator, who's charged with overseeing compliance with Title IX of the Civil Rights Act of 1964 and investigating any complaints of sex discrimination?

7. Who would a transgender student talk to if they want to transition safely in school?

8. Does the school's curriculum include issues relevant to LGBTQ+ students, especially regarding health?

9. Does the library include books and resources on LGBTQ+ issues?

10. Does the school participate in LGBTQ+ community events like Pride Day and Transgender Day of Remembrance?

If a transgender student is worried about their personal safety at school, a school administrator can describe relevant school policies and resources.

GLOSSARY

binding: The act of using restrictive clothing to bind one's breasts and create a flat appearance.

cisgender: Referring to those whose gender identity and expression align with the sex they were assigned at birth.

cissexism: The belief or assumption that cisgender people are better or more normal than transgender people.

discrimination: Unfair treatment based on factors such as a person's race, age, religion, or gender.

gender dysphoria: A medical diagnosis describing a person's emotional distress over an incongruence between their birth-assigned sex and gender identity.

gender expression: The ways in which a person expresses their gender identity, including hairstyle, clothing, makeup, voice, mannerisms, and so forth.

gender identity: Someone's internal sense of gender with regard to their self-image and ideal body and expression.

gender spectrum: A model of gender identities that some consider outdated, designed to reflect the idea that there are many gender identities outside of and in between man and woman.

gender-variant: Experiencing gender in a way that falls outside of the male-female binary.

harassment: The act of creating a hostile or unpleasant situation for someone through unwanted contact.

intersectionality: The way a person's gender, class, and race must be considered together in order to understand the oppressions they might face and the life they might lead.

intersex: Referring to people who possess any variation of genitalia or chromosomal makeup that does not fit the traditional binary of male and female.

microaggression: A casual insult to or dismissal of a member of a socially disadvantaged group. It lays bare prejudices that perpetrators may not know they have.

neurodivergent: Describing people with conditions such as depression, anxiety, autism, and schizophrenia, whose neurocognitive functioning differs from the dominant social standards that are considered "normal."

nonbinary: Referring to somebody who identifies as outside of the scope of the traditional gender binary.

passing: In the trans community, this refers to the act of someone blending in as the gender they are presenting as, without the risk of anyone seeing them as their assigned gender.

transgender: A person whose gender identity is different from that usually associated with the anatomy they were born with.

transition: The physical, mental, and social act of expressing a gender identity that does not match the one assigned at birth.

transphobia: Discrimination against transgender people.

tucking: The act of hiding traditionally male-assigned genitalia using special undergarments and other tools.

EGALE CANADA

120 Carlton Street, Suite 217
Toronto, ON M5A 4K2
Canada
(888) 204-7777
Website: *www.egale.ca*
Facebook, Instagram, and Twitter: *@EgaleCanada*
Egale Canada is an advocacy organization that works to advance equality for LGBTQ+ Canadians through research, education, awareness, and resources.

HUMAN RIGHTS CAMPAIGN

1640 Rhode Island Avenue NW
Washington, DC 20036-3278
(202) 628-4160
Website: *www.hrc.org/*
Facebook, Instagram: *@humanrightscampaign*
Twitter: *@HRC*
The Human Rights Campaign fights for LGBTQ+ rights through campaigns and programs.

NATIONAL CENTER FOR TRANSGENDER EQUALITY

1032 15th Street NW
Suite 199
Washington, D.C. 20005
(202) 642-4542
Website: *www.transequality.org*
Facebook: *@transequalitynow*
Twitter: *@TransEquality*
The National Center for Transgender Equality works to promote policies that increase understanding and acceptance of transgender people in society.

PSYCHOLOGY TODAY

115 East Twenty-Third Street, Ninth Floor
New York, NY 10010
Website: *www.psychologytoday.com*
Facebook: *@psychologytoday*
Instagram: *@psych_today*
Twitter: *@psychtoday*
Psychology Today is a magazine and online site focusing on psychology and mental health. It provides listings for mental health professionals as well as resources on issues such as dealing with gender dysphoria.

TRANSGENDER LAW CENTER

PO Box 70976
Oakland, CA 94612
(510) 587-9696
Website: *www.transgenderlawcenter.org*
Facebook, Instagram, Twitter: *@TransLawCenter*
The Transgender Law Center works to protect and advance the rights of transgender people and provides resources and education for transgender people and their allies.

TRANS LIFELINE

548 Market Street, PMB 15337
San Francisco, CA 94104
(877) 565-8860
Website: *www.translifeline.org*
Facebook, Instagram, Twitter: *@TransLifeline*
Trans Lifeline operates a 24/7 hotline for crisis assistance and provides information and resources on topics related to transgender issues.

TRANS YOUTH EQUALITY FOUNDATION

P.O. Box 201
Orono, ME 04473
(207) 478-4087
Website: *www.transyouthequality.org/*
Facebook, Instagram: *@transyouthequality*
Twitter: *@TYEFofficial*
The Trans Youth Equality Foundation provides education, advocacy, and support for transgender young people by offering resources and support services such as youth camps, educational programs, and workshops.

THE TREVOR PROJECT

PO Box 69232
West Hollywood, CA 90069
(212) 695-8650
Website: *www.thetrevorproject.org*
Facebook: *@TheTrevorProject*
Instagram and Twitter: *@TrevorProject*
The Trevor Project is a nonprofit organization that provides resources for LGBTQ+ youth including a crisis hotline, a welcoming online community, guides, and articles.

FOR FURTHER READING

Brezina, Corona. *Coming Out as Transgender*. New York, NY: Rosen Publishing, 2017.

Currie, Stephen. *LGBTQ Rights and Activism*. San Diego, CA: ReferencePoint Press, 2021.

Devor, Aaron H. *Transgender: A Reference Handbook*. Santa Barbara, CA: ABC-CLIO, 2019.

Erickson-Schroth, Laura. *Trans Bodies, Trans Selves: A Resource for the Transgender Community*. 2nd ed. New York, NY: Oxford University Press, 2022.

Hugstad, Kristi. *Be You, Only Better: Real Life Self-Care for Young Adults (and Everyone Else)*. Novato, CA: New World Library, 2021

Klein, Rebecca T. *Transgender Rights and Protections*. New York, NY: Rosen Publishing, 2017.

Landau, Jennifer. *Teens Talk About Self-Esteem and Self-Confidence*. New York, NY: Rosen Publishing, 2018.

Markey, Charlotte N. *Being You: The Body Image Book for Boys*. Cambridge, UK: Cambridge University Press, 2022.

Markey, Charlotte N. *The Body Image Book for Girls: Love Yourself and Grow Up Fearless*. Cambridge, UK: Cambridge University Press, 2021.

Meyer, Susan. *Health Issues When You're Transgender*. New York, NY: Rosen Publishing, 2017.

The New York Times Editorial Staff. *Striving for Equality*. Buffalo, NY: Rosen Publishing, 2019.

The New York Times Editorial Staff. *Transgender Activists and Celebrities*. Buffalo, NY: Rosen Publishing, 2019.

Penne, Barbra. *Transgender Role Models and Pioneers*. New York, NY: Rosen Publishing, 2017.

Skeen, Michelle. *Just as You Are: A Teen's Guide to Self-Acceptance and Lasting Self-Esteem*. Oakland, CA: New Harbinger Publications, Inc., 2018.

Woods, Sara. *Identifying as Transgender*. New York, NY: Rosen Publishing, 2017.

INDEX

M

N

P

R

S

T

U

V

ABOUT THE AUTHOR

ROSE MCCARTHY is an author who has written numerous books for children and young adults. Several have addressed social and legal issues faced by teens, including *Sexual Harassment* (Coping). She lives in New York.

PHOTO CREDITS

Photo credits: Cover, Dmytro Zinkevych/Shutterstock.com; Cover, pp. 1-80 STUDIO DREAM/Shutterstock.com; Cover, p. 1 HIGOOD/Shutterstock.com; p. 5 SrideeStudio/Shutterstock.com; p. 6 Melinda Nagy/Shutterstock.com; p. 9, 62 AlessandroBiascioli/Shutterstock.com; p. 11 Africa Studio/Shutterstock.com; p. 13 nito/Shutterstock.com; p. 15 Master1305/Shutterstock.com; p. 16 farinasfoto/Shutterstock.com; p. 19 fizkes/Shutterstock.com; p. 21 pixelheadphoto digitalskillet/Shutterstock.com; p. 23 Sabrina Bracher/Shutterstock.com; p. 25 PR Image Factory/Shutterstock.com; p. 28 VikaJpeg/Shutterstock.com; p. 30 Motortion Films/Shutterstock.com; p. 32 UfaBizPhoto/Shutterstock.com; p. 35 creo2/Shutterstock.com; p. 37 loreanto/Shutterstock.com; p. 39 Josu Ozkaritz/Shutterstock.com; p. 40 Nuva Frames/Shutterstock.com; p. 43 Millenius/Shutterstock.com; p. 45 Jaren Jai Wicklund/Shutterstock.com; p. 46 Michelle_C/Shutterstock.com; p. 47 MDV Edwards/Shutterstock.com; p. 49 DMegias/Shutterstock.com; p. 50 BAZA Production/Shutterstock.com; p. 53 SB Arts Media/Shutterstock.com; p. 55 lazyllama/Shutterstock.com; p. 57 Dina Mukhutdinova/Shutterstock.com; p. 58 romain-jorge/Shutterstock.com; p. 59 Norb_KM/Shutterstock.com; p. 61 aguscrespophoto/Shutterstock.com; p. 65 Krakenimages.com/Shutterstock.com; p. 67 wavebreakmedia/Shutterstock.com.